B[illegible]
THE SMILES:

An army veteran's wife's personal guide for supporting families suffering from PTSD

CARON SANDERS-CROOK

ISBN: 978-1-8381790-3-8

First published in 2020

Disclaimer

The views expressed within this book are the sole responsibility of the author and do not reflect the opinions of any other person, publisher, company or organisation. The author and publisher do not assume and hereby disclaim any liability to any party for any loss, damage, or disruption caused by errors or omissions, whether such errors or omissions result from negligence, accident, or any other cause. This book is not intended as a substitute for the advice of medical professionals, including mental health professionals. The reader should regularly consult a health professional in matters relating to his/her health, and particularly with respect to any symptoms that may require diagnosis, medical or psychological attention.

For a FREE sheet of

High Touch Jin Shin (acupressure)

"finger holds"

Please contact me at

Behind.the.smilesPTSD@gmail.com

To Mark, Charlotte, and Gareth.

Thank you for the joy, the laughter, and the learning.

I Love You

Contents

PREFACE

Hello, and thank you for picking up a copy of this guide. Writing and publishing my own book is certainly one thing off my bucket list, although I would never have guessed that my first book would be about Post Traumatic Stress Disorder (PTSD)! Before we begin, please permit me to share a little bit about myself:

I had an exciting childhood. Growing up in Bewdley, I was bullied at school because of the skin I am in, and my parents split up when I was young. I never felt like I belonged. I understood little about my heritage or background, as this was rarely discussed in those days. However, one thing I always knew was that I wanted to be a "magic nurse". I wanted to help people, healing and making them better, and I would constantly dream and fantasise about doing so. With this in mind, it's little wonder that I pursued medicine, first training as a nurse and then qualifying in the practise and teaching of several complementary therapies.

During my nurse training and for the first twelve months after, I was taken under the wing of a fantastic nurse who saw potential in me. Des mentored me through every step of my training, teaching me patient care and improving my medical skill. At the time I was suffering through an abusive and miserable marriage, and her support proved invaluable. She stood by me during the divorce, and ultimately presented me with an opportunity to join the Queen Alexandra's Royal Army Nursing Corps. At first, I was reluctant; joining the army would be a huge and wholly unexpected change, but Des persuaded me:

"Go for it," she said. "Go live your dream and travel the world, you have nothing to keep you here; this is your second chance." After signing up at the nearest Army Careers office, and being posted to Aldershot, Germany, The Gulf, and finally Colchester, I served for approximately six years. During that time, I met Mark, to whom I have now been married for over thirty years. In those days, postings did not benefit married personnel, and we were constantly separated, posted at opposite corners of the globe. Ultimately, I chose love, leaving my own position and travelling as an army wife with Mark and our two children, until he finished his twenty-two-year career. Whilst travelling, I continued to study and nurse at various medical centres and hospitals, achieving my BSc (Hons) in Health and Social Care with the Open University, as well as other professional and therapeutic qualifications.

When Mark left the army, we settled on the Essex coast with our children and our Saint Bernard dogs. I had always wanted to live by the sea; it was especially dear to us since we got married near the coast.

I focused my career in the social care sector, managing and turning around distressed care homes, holding various positions – from operations manager to roles in quality and governance. I loved working with people, not only treating them but guiding, coaching and helping them develop. As I continued to train in delivering various therapies, I began to gather a client-base and had a small practice alongside my main job. I created, researched, and developed my own complementary therapy, which is gentle yet extremely powerful. The feedback from those who received it was terrific, and I owe a huge thanks to those people for acting as my "guinea pigs". This therapy will form the subject matter for another book, so keep your eyes peeled!

As I continued with my career, I began to notice changes in Mark's behaviour. He became distant from us, and threw himself into his work. Ultimately, after seeing a specialist, he was diagnosed with Post Traumatic Stress Disorder. This did not really come as a surprise, given the colourful and extensive military career he'd had. However, I was not ready for the impact it would have on him, and on our family. There are many organisations out there who provide support for PTSD, but the glossy images they display are some distance from the truth. Despite trawling websites and directories, joining social media groups, and sending out multiple emails and telephone calls, I found it extremely challenging to access support, both for me and for my family as a whole. I wanted positive outcomes from things that people had tried, not just sympathy or empathy.

For this reason, I ultimately decided to carry out my own SurveyMonkey questionnaire, to find out how other families were coping with this perceived lack of information. I called my survey *You, Me and PTSD*, and the results were very interesting:

- 43% of respondents were receiving help for PTSD symptoms themselves.
- 42% of respondents were unsure of where to seek help or advice on PTSD.
- 45% of respondents said they had not been able to access support or help in a timely way, and that there had been delays within the process.
- 86% of those respondents supporting someone living with PTSD were not receiving or were not able to access support for themselves, either quickly or at a time that worked for them.
- 71% of respondents said that PTSD had visibly affected those around them. 29% said they were not sure.
- 70% of respondents said they were not veterans themselves, but they were supporting someone. 30% said they were veterans.

Lots of information came back to me from the organisations I approached, telling me how I could support Mark and help him manage his PTSD, but nothing for us **as a family**. I knew how to help him cope; I had been doing it for years. What I needed was advice and guidance for myself and my children, to help us emotionally deal with the day-to-day behaviours and changes we were seeing. Despite multiple requests, I received nothing; some websites did not even respond to my email. From all this, it was hard not to draw the conclusion that there is simply limited information available to help families cope with PTSD. I don't blame the organisations in question for this, and I have no doubt that in future there will be a significant improvement on this front, as it becomes clearer that PTSD not only impacts the sufferer but those around them too. So, if this book raises awareness and enables organisations to communicate better with families, then I will have achieved my aim.

Whilst studying my management degree, I discovered the joy of journaling. Journaling was a way of bearing my soul, pouring my emotions and frustrations onto the page. It was therapeutic, confidential, and helped me to manage my feelings. When you write things down, the emotions stay on the page, and this created a dynamic where I could gain perspective and cope better. *Behind The Smiles* is born out of my journaling.

There are many textbooks available which explain PTSD, the symptoms and causes, but what these books lack is a personal touch. This book is written from my experience, in my own words, and includes real stories of how PTSD impacted my family. Reading this may be difficult for some of you, I know, especially since many of my experiences might match with your own. With this in mind, it's okay to "thumb through" and dive in where you feel most comfortable, and at the parts that resonate most with you. If you want to go back over the other chapters at a different time, or start at the beginning and work your way through, that's fine too. Ultimately, you will get the best out of this book by taking it at your own pace, being open-minded, and having a journal or notebook to write in.

I hope that my experiences and my coping strategies will help you or your loved ones to cope with PTSD, and I'm honoured that you've chosen this book as a way forward. May it bring you the peace and the bravery to reach out and seek the nurturing you so deserve.

I would love to hear about your experiences. You can contact me at behind.the.smilesptsd@gmail.com

CHAPTER 1
INTRODUCTION

"Life has many ways of testing a person's will, either by having nothing happen at all or by having everything happen all at once."

Paulo Coelho

Before I share my full story, I'd like to show you how to make the best possible use of this book. As mentioned, this book was born as a result of my journaling. My aim is to help you see that you are not alone in dealing with the impact of PTSD, and that there are strategies out there which can help not only the sufferer, but also those suffering alongside them.

As you read through the chapters, some symbols will ask you to think and reflect, make notes, and invite you to take care of yourself – using my tried and tested techniques. I still use these techniques today, so I am confident they will help you too. Look out for the following:

This symbol invites you to think about highlighted issues and what you might do about them.

This symbol invites you to make a note.

This symbol invites you to carry out the exercise next to it, as an element of self-care. Your loved one or friend can also do this if they wish.

I hope you find the information in this book useful, relevant and thought-provoking, as I invite you to stop for a moment and be present with what you are experiencing. Whether it's you, a loved one, or a friend who is living with PTSD, I have first-hand experience in dealing with the fallout of this condition, **and** first-hand experience of how the tips in this book can change your relationship for the better.

I want to be clear that these are my experiences, thoughts, rants, and solutions, and they are not a replacement for professional help. I would urge anyone who needs it to seek professional support; at the back of this book I have included some useful contacts, so you can do just that.

Now, find a quiet space, grab a cuppa, a notebook and pen, and get comfy as I share my story with you.

POEM PTSD

PTSD and this dreaded anxiety,
Caused by stressful, frightening or distressing events,
Can affect anyone, not just people playing soldiers
and living in tents.
The flashbacks, nightmares, painful images and sensations,
Suffered by those who gave to different nations.

The feeling sick, the trembling, the sweating, and the pain,
You have to ask yourself – what was there really to gain?
The guilt, the wonder, and the shame,
How did I get drawn into your dangerous game?
The avoidance, the isolation, the emotional numb,
I know how this happened, I'm not entirely dumb.

Now I'm broken, I'm angry, I can't sleep.
The visions, the triggers, the nausea is mine to keep.
Do I drink or take drugs to make it go away?
I might even talk to someone, just for today.

I need to find me, the laughter, the joy,
The fun I would have as a girl or a boy.
So, help me please, I'm screaming inside,
I'm scared of the world, so I try to hide.

Come find me, reach out and offer a hand.
Please help me, I've given so much for this land.

Caron Sanders-Crook

CHAPTER 2
TRIGGERS

"Time flies over us, but leaves its shadow behind."

Nathaniel Hawthorne

The triggers for PTSD can come in many forms. They can be sights, sounds, smells, thoughts, clothes, or even just a familiar look or action from an otherwise oblivious person. Mark's triggers were mostly related to smell. For example, the smell of fuel led to a distressing incident at a gas station, which will later form an important part of this story. Often, sounds would trigger him too, making him jump or stop in his tracks. In many cases, I would watch him mentally "transport" to another place and time, before bringing himself back and carrying on.

When we talked about these experiences, he would share with me what he saw, and what his surroundings were like. Although in some ways I could understand what he was describing - as I had been with him to many of those past places - I could not relate to what he was experiencing in that moment. Mentally, I had moved on from our life in the armed forces.

Once a PTSD sufferer's memories or experiences are activated, they often begin a spiral, with other triggers being activated one after the other - until the person is actually reliving the past situation for real. I have seen this happen with my husband. As their emotional state heightens, hypersensitivity is induced, increasing to such a pitch that someone or something needs to interfere and break the cycle.

When it comes to my husband, provided I have the energy and insight, I will step in to try and break the cycle myself.

Sometimes my input has little effect. I cannot always "reach" him, as there are times when he is too far in. Sometimes his own body intervenes, and he burns himself out to the extent that he becomes ill, and has to take to his bed for a few days. Thankfully this does not happen very often, but I do feel for him when it does.

Mark's PTSD is usually triggered at times of high stress, generally with his work, which involves medical logistics and providing medical cover to remote areas. Most of the pressure is self-induced, as he will not let his colleagues help him. One of the problems with having PTSD is that sufferers are often unable to perceive what is needed. In my husband's case, he wants to maintain control of what is going on around him. From his perspective, accepting help would only make him more vulnerable.

Often, Mark and I have conversations about help and support. We talk about coping strategies, things he can do while he's alone, ways that he can manage his triggers without spiralling. We normally agree on solutions, and for a short while things improve, before eventually going back to exactly how they were before. Ultimately, my husband is more comfortable with what he knows, and prefers to stay in that comfort zone. However, I can of course appreciate that it is difficult to dictate your own wants and needs when you're in someone else's company, especially when that person is your closest ally.

Whatever the situation, it is often difficult for people to express that they feel vulnerable and out of control, and this is particularly hard in times of crisis. Furthermore, talking is generally easier for women than it is for men, and I often feel that this is a hindrance when dealing with something as powerful as PTSD. Talking-therapy can work wonders, but actually instigating this therapy is another matter entirely. During therapy sessions, we have discussed the idea of Mark giving up his current job, but he loves it. Asking him to retire, especially when he feels that he has so much left to give, is extremely difficult. Later in this book I will discuss the impact that PTSD has on the body, and the chemical changes which take place in a sufferer's brain and body.

Before Mark attended residentials - which is my nickname for Combat Stress therapy - I had some idea of what his triggers were, but my understanding was limited. I knew that loud, unexpected noises could set him off. Likewise, we generally avoided shopping at the busiest times. He'd stopped drinking, in order to maintain self-awareness. All in all, things seemed to be well under control, until a significant event in London left us all reeling. As the triggers started to take hold, more and more signs and symptoms of PTSD crept into our lives. At points, things were almost unbearable, but as a family we have pulled together and stuck it out.

Even after all this time, I still don't know every single trigger, but I do know the ones which invoke the most significant reaction in my husband. This I have learned through hard work and perseverance, and I hope that you can do the same for your loved one.

- Think for a moment. What triggers have you identified? Have there been any significant changes that may have set the triggers off?
- What have you noticed about yourself, how do you respond to those situations?
- Make a note of anything you have noticed.

CHAPTER 3
ANXIETY, FEAR, ANGER

"Where there is anger, there is always pain underneath."

Eckhart Tolle

The earliest signs of Mark's PTSD were anxiety, fear, and anger. He would swing from being completely quiet, to being anxious and jumpy about everything, before becoming tearful and then angry. The anxiety would manifest in the smallest ways. For example, if I said I was going to clean a paw print off the wall (I have lots of paw prints on a wall in the house because our dogs sleep upside down and rest their paws on it - big dogs!) he would keep mentioning it and badgering me until I had done it. Then, when that job was complete, he would be on to the next small thing and continuously badger me to do that too. This quickly became exhausting, especially when I had many other things on my list, and was working to my sequence of completion, not his. To add to this, his anxiety perspective seemed unbalanced. While the smaller things took on enormous importance, matters of priority - like checking the gas cooker to make sure it was switched off - did not seem to feature.

Fear would show itself in Mark's body language. At times, he would look like he was retreating or cowering, trying to hide himself from the world. Sometimes he would say 'I feel scared,' without knowing what he was afraid of. Often, these episodes manifested as a result of nightmares. We've all had dreams where you wake up feeling as if the incident actually happened, and for a sufferer of PTSD these dreams and their after-effects can be particularly vivid. Mark would constantly feel as if something terrible was going to happen. While I tried to remain positive, it was difficult; one of the hardest things about living with PTSD is trying to anticipate what will happen next, when the next incident will occur, and how you and your family will deal with it.

While my husband's anxiety and the fear were somewhat manageable, his anger was a real concern. Up until that point we had hardly ever argued, but now I could feel the tension between us growing. This was exasperated by Mark's lack of physical activity. Previously, he'd played rugby, which provided an outlet, but now that he'd stopped training and playing there was nowhere else for these feelings to go. There is a great deal of science about pent up anger and the damage it can do to the body, and this worried me. I knew that there had to be an outlet, and I worried about when and how it would show itself. My own frustrations were growing too. I simply didn't know whether to stick or twist in any given moment, and I was constantly questioning whether I should do nothing, or do something.

Things only got worse when our son moved to the USA. As Mark later told me, he felt better when our son was around, because if anything did happen then he would have someone to "lean on". Now, his anxiety was heightened, increased by the fear of losing control. For me, it was like watching a movie without sound. I felt as if I were on the periphery, trying to interpret the situation and emotions that caused such behaviour, without having any clue of the storyline or plot. I knew that I had to take some lesson from this, but what was it? It was no good asking Mark what I could do to help him, because he himself did not know or understand what was happening.

Each morning, I would ask the same question: 'How are you today?' In response, I'd get the same message back: 'Let's just take one day at a time.' I would listen, listen, listen, just happy for him to share any clues that might help us to overcome this. We would always try to end the conversation by moving forward, doing as he said, taking one day at a time. 'What now?' I'd ask, or 'What are you planning on doing today?' It might be that he would take the dogs for a walk, or meet up with a friend to talk, both of which would raise his spirits a little.

While Mark was out, I generally took the opportunity to do something I loved. Not just because I felt as if it was important for me to enjoy myself, but also to keep my mind off the situation. Whether it involved playing gongs, meditating, or going for a walk, I did things that kept me connected and fed my spirituality. I found that if I didn't do this, I became fearful and anxious on Mark's behalf. Like attracts like, after all. I had become so used to my husband's fear and anxiety that I was beginning to live in the same bubble. Likewise, our daughter also became worried, anticipating what might happen if we all went out together.

Whilst Mark was attending residentials, my daughter and I would talk openly. We both acknowledged that there was now a behavioural pattern developing, with each of us going through similar preparation routines in order to try and anticipate how Mark might behave. We had walked on eggshells for so long that we were now anticipating and responding to things that had not yet happened.

Together, my daughter and I decided we would take a step back - becoming watchers rather than responders. It was Mark's experience, not ours. We could not and would not take responsibility or ownership for his PTSD. If we continued to do this, we would only perpetuate the cycle of anxiety, stress, and fear. We had to think about how our actions would best help and support him. My husband needed positivity, not negativity, and involving ourselves too closely in the process of dealing with PTSD was only dragging us down too, lowering everybody's mood. I have always believed that creating positivity and positive space is essential. Focus on what you want, not on what you don't want. I needed to be more mindful of me.

One of the ways I did this, was to check myself whenever I found that I was getting too involved. I used a calming meditation, in addition to my morning and evening meditation, to make sure this happened. I have included this in the hope that it may also help you. It does not take long, and you can practise it almost anywhere.

Centering, Calming Breath

Find a quiet spot where you will not be disturbed. It might be a place in your home or even outdoors. Turn off your phone, and if there are people at home, tell them you are seeking some quiet time.

Make yourself comfortable. Sit or lie down, close your eyes and take some deep, slow, gentle, cleansing and calming breaths.

Breathe in until the count of 7, and out for the count of 7. If this is not comfortable, try taking shorter breaths.

Do this at least 3 times or until you feel a sense of peace inside you.

Place your hands on your heart area.

Now focus your breathing on the heart area, as if you are breathing in and out of your heart.

Picture a memory or visualise a special time, place or person, and focus on this while breathing.

Keep this in your mind's eye.

Notice the feeling you get from visualising it. If you cannot imagine it, then sense it – feel it, and the joy it brings.

What is it about this image or feeling that brings you joy?

Focus on this.

Make it bigger, brighter and expand the energy, so it fills your whole body and beyond.

Keep making it bigger, until it fills the room you are in. Expand the energy far outside of your body, so it surrounds you.

Build an imaginary bubble around yourself, and check that it is full of this lovely energy you have just created. Embrace the feeling of building and filling it even more.

Breathe in the positivity, and breathe out the positivity, filling your bubble until it's bulging. Give it a colour if you wish.

Sit in your space for a while. Set the intention that this radiant energy will penetrate every single cell within you.

Keep this going for as long as you need to (you will know when to move on).

When you are ready, set the intention to carry this energy with you for the rest of the day.

Take a few deep, gentle, cleansing breaths. Now, slowly open your eyes and take in your surroundings.

Savour the energy you have just experienced.

As I began to step back and focus my attention more on a positive living experience, things began to change for the better. As I looked around me at my home, and what we had achieved together, I started once again to become more appreciative of what I had, what we had. I had to focus and build on this.

- Think for a moment. What examples of anxiety, fear and anger come to mind? What have you noticed in your loved one? Can you sense or pick up when the person is experiencing this?
- What is the behaviour you are seeing? What have you noticed about yourself?
- Make a note in your journal or notebook.

CHAPTER 4
NIGHTMARES AND SLEEP DISTURBANCES

"Even in his sleep, he couldn't escape."

Madeleine Roux

Prior to Mark's PTSD, I usually went to bed before him, and this is still the case today. As I've mentioned, Mark had played rugby for most of his life, and therefore a few broken noses have contributed to intense bouts of snoring. I know for sure that there will be husbands and wives out there reading this who have experienced something similar! In those days, it wasn't just the snoring either. Mark's nightmares were fairly frequent, leading to traumatic episodes, and therefore I always wanted to make sure I got at least some sleep prior to these happening.

Due to his tiredness, Mark would sleep quite a lot - both throughout the day and in the early evening. On some occasions, I actually saw him fall asleep in the middle of typing an email. At first we had a laugh about this, but I soon realised it was a sign and symptom of something more serious, and became quite worried. He also suffered from sleep apnoea, and continues to until this day, which made the sleep incidents more distressing.

As you might have guessed, having a good night's sleep at that point was very hit-and-miss for Mark. I actually developed quite a sixth sense for whether it was going to be a good night, or whether he was going to have a nightmare. As someone who does a lot of energy work, I could feel this quite acutely. The energy in the room would darken, and the vibrational level would drop. The easiest way to describe it, is to imagine that you are in a room where the temperature suddenly falls. When you become alert to this, you can feel a tangible difference in the air, and in the room's energy. When my husband's breathing changed, my "spidey" senses would be on high alert. Even if I was in a deep sleep, I was so tuned into the process that I would just wake up anyway, waiting to see if it would fade, or whether I'd need to intervene and wake Mark up. Most of the time, after waking, Mark would be unable to talk for a while. He would just say, 'That was f***** horrible!' and sit staring into space, trying to erase the images left behind from his nightmare.

In order to gauge how bad the night might be, I created a mental graphic equaliser. I noted Mark's breathing, the number of times he would shout or talk, and what tone he used. His body movement was a good indicator. Did he toss and turn or just twitch every now and again? Sometimes he would literally jump off the bed and back onto it in the same spot, as if he had been lifted and dropped. On the next page I have included a diagram of my mental graphic equaliser, to demonstrate better what I mean.

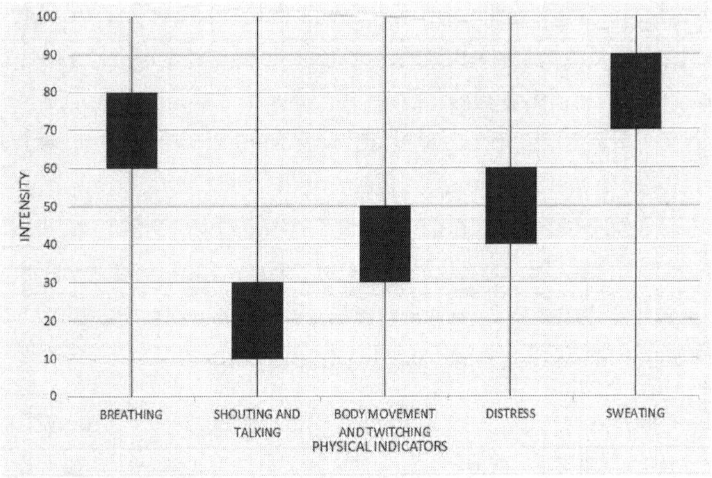

My 'Alert' Graphic Equaliser

Each of these elements would fluctuate depending on what Mark would be experiencing. The levels did not have to be close to 10 – it would very much depend on the combination of indicators and the level of distress I felt he was experiencing. Occasionally, Mark would just sit bolt upright, as if he'd shocked himself out of it, but normally I would have to wake him up. If I was away, and one of the kids went to wake him, they knew only to wake him from the feet. I myself learned this the hard way, by getting caught in a stranglehold. Interesting, but not fun!

Night Sweats

We've all had bad dreams, where you wake up sweating with fear. In your mind, what you dreamt was so real, and you can still feel the emotions attached to that episode. Well, multiply that by 100 and you might be somewhere close to what Mark was experiencing. As a family, we've had to replace countless sheets, pillows and mattresses, all as a result of night sweats. At first I kept telling Mark to visit the GP, I thought his menopause was worse than mine! I've never had night sweats or hot flushes as bad as that; he would be literally dripping. It's true that Mark has always been a hot person at night (no not like that, not for this book anyway!); I used to call him my human radiator, as he was great for snuggling up to on winter nights. This, however, was ridiculous. There were occasions where, when he did wake up in the middle of the night, he would just immediately jump in the shower - there was that much sweat. We considered plastic covers for the pillows and mattresses, but in reality this would only have made things worse, ruining the chance of a good night's sleep altogether.

There were times when I did and still do consider the idea of sleep divorce - where a married couple sleep in different beds and separate rooms. But, I couldn't bring myself to do it. After all, contact and sharing close proximity are rare. So, I soldiered on, snatching the few really good nights of sleep possible, struggling through the sweats and the nightmares.

Flashbacks

As any person living with PTSD will know, flashbacks are as real as they can be. When a sufferer experiences a flashback, they are back in the moment, reliving the experience all over again. It was normally evident to me when Mark was having a flashback, as he would just freeze on the spot, staring or dipping his head. Sometimes, he would just carry on with what he was doing, and at other times he would need to take himself away for a moment. Regardless of whether he stayed put, or moved to a quiet spot, I could tell that something had happened. The experience would generally lead to a night of nightmares and terrors, but there was really no pattern to it. Sometimes we would be driving, and he would describe to me what he was seeing as clearly as if it were right in front of him, relaying the locations, the incident, and what had happened. Other times, it was unclear, almost foggy - like waking from a dream.

Mark's flashbacks also had an impact on who he felt he could and couldn't trust. If someone reminded him of a certain person or negative association, he would not and could not connect with them. Sometimes he would be able to explain this to me, and at other times he couldn't - as with everything it largely depended on the day.

Night-time flashbacks were just as vivid and graphical, some in colour and some in black and white. The more graphic ones resulted in Mark getting up and going downstairs. He found that changing his location broke the image connection. If he did not do this, and just tried to go back to sleep, he usually went straight back into the flashback, starting from where he'd left off. During these experiences, he would be sweating, breathing fast and shaking. His appearance dramatically changed - he looked distressed, horrified. It was frightening to see, but extremely fascinating at the same time.

- Think about a time when your loved one had sleepless nights, nightmares, or flashbacks. Were these linked to the mood they were in during the day, or something they may have seen on the TV? Were they related to food? Or were they connected to something they experienced on a personal level?

- Keep a diary note of when these incidents occur, and see if you can link them to anything.

- Have you identified any factors that make you alert to the possibility of a restless night? What would you put in the graphic equaliser?

- Make a note of anything you feel is significant.

CHAPTER 5
SIGNS AND SYMPTOMS OF DEPRESSION

"There are some things about myself I can't explain to anyone. There are some things I don't understand at all."

Haruki Murakami

Mark and I used to love going out together, whether it was exploring, meeting friends or just visiting places we loved. As the PTSD took hold, this happened less and less. He stopped playing rugby, and on some days he would barely speak to anyone. There were occasions when every time I walked into the room, he would leave. Naturally, I started to question myself. What was I doing wrong? Was he having an affair? It seemed as if the only thing he could relate to was his phone. Even when we went away together, he hardly spoke to me. The kids were ignored, and there was a total loss of interest in anything going on at home. Instead, he just clung to his work, burying his head in it. Only our dogs, two beautiful St Bernards, kept the connection between us as a family. Jeeves and Worcester, and before them Henry, got my husband out of bed every morning, and helped him to face the world. Animals are intelligent, they knew that he had changed, and kept him laughing by doing foolish things. Thank God for our pets – as a family we owe them so much.

Jeeves and Worcester

Our beloved Henry

As Mark's interest began to dwindle even further, it wasn't long before the full extent of his isolation and withdrawal became apparent. He would go to work, walk and feed the dogs, and that was it. It became much more difficult to persuade him to help around the house. He would just say, 'It's fine, the house is fine.' It drove me mad. I just had to do what I could during the week, and would then spend most of my weekends cleaning and tidying until I eventually ran out of steam. I tried to stay positive, but every now and then the situation got the better of me, and I would question and moan about why this was happening. I knew that I needed to find a solution, to at least try and find something positive in all the extra housework. So, I started downloading music, and doing the chores whilst rocking out and dancing around the house. I've always loved dancing, so I thought why not incorporate it into my daily routine? I would wait until Mark went out with the dogs, and then have a "cleaning disco". Of course, whilst this made things better for me, Mark was only getting worse. Everything felt like such an effort for him. I now understand that he was just exhausted, trying to cope in the best way he could.

As discussed earlier, the sleep changes and concentration problems were, to me, significant symptoms of depression. Mark's self-worth and self-esteem were low, and he was frequently tearful, which was highly unusual. He gained weight, and his eating habits changed. He was eating junk food and biscuits by the barrel. He began to feel low and complain of aches and pains. To some extent, I expected the aches and pains, as he had played rugby for most of his childhood and adult life. The difference, however, was that he had never previously complained about these. Even if his leg was hanging off, he would still put his boots on and act like nothing was wrong! Now though, things had changed. Someone who had always been the life and soul of the party, full of energy and laughs, was shutting down. It was as if his light had gone out; the symptoms of PTSD began to feed into one another, creating a person whom I did not recognise and did not have anything in common with. The void between us felt greater than ever before.

- Make a note of any signs and symptoms you have identified in your loved one. Is it time to seek professional help?
- How are you feeling? What have you noticed about your mood and interaction with others?
- What can you help them to focus on, to make life “lighter and brighter”, and to increase positivity?

CHAPTER 6
HOW PTSD AFFECTED US

"Let everything happen to you, beauty and terror. Just keep going, no feeling is final."

Rainer Maria Rilke

When a friend or loved one is suffering from PTSD, you will inevitably spend a lot of time covering for them. Whether that means making excuses to your children about why their father isn't around, or to your friends about why you can't go out tonight, unfortunately this is a common occurrence, and something I've had to deal with in spades. But you can't hide it forever. Every year the symptoms were getting more and more complex. Our kids aren't stupid, they understood that something was very wrong, and eventually I did have to sit them down and explain that Mark was not well. In doing so, I worked with my limited knowledge, to try and explain the behaviours they were seeing. The situation had a huge impact on who they could bring home, and when it was safe to bring people over to the house. While it wasn't dangerous, I didn't know how Mark would react to having someone he didn't know in the house, and I didn't want visitors to end up in a situation where they felt uncomfortable. Inevitably, this led to losing touch with many people, including my extended family, our friends, and the kids' friends. But, we just had to get on with life.

During this period, it became apparent to me that, as a family, we were traumatised by what we were going through. I was constantly putting on a brave face, but my patience had reached its limits. There were times when we were out with friends, and Mark would just fall asleep at the table. It was embarrassing and rude. I knew he couldn't help it, but I was just so fed up. I was exhausted, physically and emotionally.

Everything he was going through, I was now experiencing too: the withdrawal, the isolation, the bad nights, sleeplessness. But I had to keep going; work was my outlet and my sanctuary. Unfortunately, my manager at the time was not helpful at all. When I told this person about Mark's PTSD, they started to performance-manage me. Oh, and they were ex-military. Go figure! Eventually that manager left, and I got a new boss, as you do, also ex-forces. This one is an absolute bloody star and has been supportive, understanding and very hard-working. I was given the time and space I needed to get through the crisis, time to recuperate and re-energise, and I am and always will be eternally grateful.

Speaking to other people about PTSD is always tricky. For example, if your partner is having an affair, people are sympathetic; everyone has an opinion and advice to offer. They will sit and listen and feel sorry for you. If your partner has PTSD, people just don't know what to say. They don't know how to react; often they'll try to change the subject and avoid the topic altogether. I don't blame them for this. It's down to a lack of knowledge and understanding about the condition – people don't want to make things worse by saying the wrong thing. Of course, I did try to explain, but I am not sure how much people really understood. And how could they, really? There was no reason for them to know about PTSD, or the effect it was having on our family.

That being said, I do not feel the reactions of certain people helped the situation. While our extended family had sympathy, they were initially in denial, and it is my opinion that their doubts played a big role in Mark not seeking professional help earlier. He would make inroads, agreeing to get support, only to be told by people that his behaviour was probably down to some other medical ailment, such as high blood pressure. A person suffering from PTSD needs to be loved and reassured that it is okay not to be okay, and that there's nothing wrong with seeking help. It takes enormous courage to admit to yourself that you need assistance, and to give yourself permission to be vulnerable.

As I've mentioned, finding support for my family was extremely difficult. All the programmes were set up purely to support the sufferer, rather than their loved ones. So, I decided to study and research myself, embarking on a crisis counselling course which would help me to support Mark and the family better, along with starting a course which included one-to-one counselling sessions.

From a very young age I've had to stand tall, on my own two feet, and this was no different. I mean no disrespect to Mark here, but I'm sure he would agree that even before the PTSD, he was never there for me in times of need or crisis. Instead, he was usually away on operational duty. I knew how to dig deep, how to keep smiling and carry on. I don't crumble easily, and I was determined to stick it out. I trust in the "Multiverse", and to this end every challenge that we have faced has been overcome. So, I knew that the right outcome would show itself, even if it took time. As I write this, Mark is going through a second residential with Combat Stress, a charity who provide mental health treatment for veterans. So, there is a light at the end of the tunnel. It's tough, and it takes a considerable amount of bravery to look inwards and open your own "Pandora's Box", but the light is there. My husband did not ask for this, we did not ask for this, but we will get through it together.

If your loved one is going through a Combat Stress programme, or indeed any kind of programme, give them space. If they want to open up, they will. If not, let them be. Don't probe, they are working through their coping strategies in their own way. Give them the time and space to see if the strategies work, and implement them on a personal level. Initially, the medication prescribed by such programmes can throw the person off a bit, as it impacts cognitive ability. When Mark first started with his medication he would forget things, behave oddly, and act in irrational ways, in addition to what he was already doing as a result of PTSD. This is where you need to be patient – knowing that they are doing something to try and make the experience better for them, not for you. They have to be selfish. My husband has given everything to make the world a safer and better place, and now it's his turn to receive care and kindness. As an ex-army nurse, I am well placed to help him with this, and I've started the process of re-connecting Mark with things he loves. For example, in 2019 we started camping. This really brought us all together and embraced Mark's love for the great outdoors. Then it began to rain, non-stop. Do you remember the end of 2019? The beautiful English winter: it rained, and it rained, and it rained. We are now in June and dealing with Coronavirus, and it's still raining! So, for the time being we are stuck indoors, again!

- How has PTSD affected you and your relationships? What feelings does it generate in you? Make a note in your journal or notebook.
- What can you do to try and improve the situation for yourself?
- Who can help you with this?

CHAPTER 7
AVOIDANCE AND EMOTIONAL NUMBING

"The greatest healing therapy is friendship and love."

Hubert H Humphrey

Avoidance and emotional numbing are part and parcel of PTSD. The sufferer's senses are overloaded, and the body is working in a state of heightened awareness. For most people, this is just too much to deal with. In Mark's case, he would avoid physical contact with me, especially at night. There were less cuddles, and the sexual connection would always end in, 'I'm sorry.' You can see why I thought he might be having an affair. It felt to me as if he would rather lie than have to commit to being in my company. We drifted further and further apart, until it eventually reached the point where I couldn't take it anymore. I felt as if I was failing. I couldn't cope with the silence and the sickness and the tension that went with it. I couldn't cope with the idea of having a failed marriage – I myself came from a broken home and I didn't want that for my kids. I'd had enough. So, one morning, I told Mark he needed to move out. His response was very matter-of-fact. He simply said that he agreed, and that he understood. It was as if he were going through the motions, I would have got a similar response just from asking him to buy a load of bread.

Following this, I walked out of the door and made the eighty-mile journey to my workplace. On the way, I kept going over things in my head. My heart was breaking, as if someone had damaged my very soul. I'd travelled with this man for well over ten years, given up my career and my dreams to support him. *This is how he repays me,* I kept thinking, *after all these years.*

The moment I arrived into work, I burst into tears. I was shaking; my mind was in turmoil and my heart was in pain. After I sat down with one of my managers, I decided to get back in the car and go home, to sort out the storm I'd created. It was time to put things right.

We sat down away from home at the back of the rugby club. I needed clear and honest answers, and I was going to get them. Mark swore he would never have an affair. In my heart, I knew he was telling the truth, but PTSD messes with your family dynamics and values. It turns your loved ones against you, and you against them. We discussed, at length, all of the behaviours Mark was displaying – the lies, the lack of affection, the mood swings, everything. Still, no explanation was forthcoming – he just sat there and cried. The silence only wound me up even more, I couldn't stand it. It's only now, looking back, that I realise how desperately low he was. He would have said and done anything to make himself feel better and worthy. But, at that time, I couldn't comprehend all the strange and irrational behaviour. So, I set him an ultimatum. He could come home, but only if he promised to seek help. I wasn't giving up – I knew that it was my mission to heal the void that had been created, to align our souls once again. Still though, I felt awful adding a condition to our relationship. We had never done that before. Mark and I were free spirits, a couple yes, but never losing our independence or individuality. But this was the only way forward. We couldn't carry on as we were.

It's important to understand that when your loved one starts treatment for PTSD, they won't get better immediately. There is no magic, one-size-fits-all cure for the condition, and you must still be prepared for difficult or traumatic incidents. One such incident occurred at a petrol station, when we went to visit our son in the USA. Mark had recently been on a two-week residential, where they started him on medication. I must say that I never know whether he is taking his medication regularly or not. If that sounds surprising, the truth is that he is an adult – I'm not his mother, and as an ex-medic you would assume he knows what he's doing. On occasion, I would ask how the medicine made him feel:

'Numb,' he said.

'Oh great, more numbness,' I replied.

He would then start to laugh. 'I'll be more numb than a big bang of numb things.'

Yes, you start laughing at the most bizarre things on this PTSD journey!

Anyway, back to the gas station (she says in her best American accent). Mark had booked the biggest SUV known to man; god only knows why – it was practically a monster truck. Halfway through our stay, out on the road, we ran out of gas. So, we pulled in for a top-up. Mark got out and looked at the pumps: four nozzles with numbers on. He stood and looked, and looked some more, then said, 'I don't know which one it is.'

I laughed, 'Open the petrol cap, it will say on the inside like it does for cars in the UK.'

'It doesn't, I don't know which one,' he replied, 'it doesn't say.'

I got out of the car and walked around to the pumps. 'They're all the same fuel, just different grades, right? Let's ask inside.'

'I don't know, I don't know which one it is,' Mark repeated.

I looked at him, and it suddenly dawned on me that this was not a typical gas pump dilemma. I could sense the anxiety rising and the panic setting in as he looked at me, the pumps and the cashier booth. He started waving his arms around, pacing back and forth.

Trying to rectify the situation, I immediately went inside and spoke to the cashier, who explained all about the pumps and the fuel. On her part, she seemed to find our dilemma mildly amusing, and we both laughed as she pointed out that we could use any of the pumps to fill our vehicle.

By the time I got back, however, Mark was in quite a state. He was pacing back and forth, something clearly going on in his head.

'It doesn't matter,' I said, 'we can use any of them.'

'But which one is it?' he said, raising his voice.

'I just asked,' I replied, 'it doesn't matter.'

Wanting to avoid a scene, I picked up the pump and started filling the car. Mark was spiralling again, getting redder and redder in the face, muttering about how he did not know which one it was. *We need to get out of here,* I thought.

While I was refuelling, Mark screwed up his face. He glared at me. 'And you can drive the f***** car back.'

Without saying another word, I finished refuelling, paid the cashier, and got back into the car. Inwardly, I was raging. *You chose a f***** monster truck, left-hand drive, another side of the road and now you're throwing a f***** tantrum over fuel. Are you kidding me?* As I got into the driver's seat, I kept reminding myself that I was strong, I could do this, no matter what Mark said next. I adjusted my mirror, and glanced at my son in the backseat, who was wondering what the hell he had just witnessed.

'Buckle up, baby,' I said.

Luckily, when I took the wheel, it broke the tension somewhat. Mark was sitting next to me, with his head in his hands. I just said nothing. He didn't speak to me properly for about two days after that. And yes, that hurt, but ultimately I'd coped with another unpredictable and eventful situation – and that was something to be proud of. So, the moral of the story here is: if you go abroad, make sure your vehicle is full of fuel before someone with PTSD gets in, especially if they are the main driver! And for god's sake, don't let your husband rent a monster truck!

I don't blame Mark for what happened that day. Ultimately, he was way out of his comfort zone, it was a bit too much. We've never really discussed the incident in detail. Mark and I skated around each other for a while, making small talk, and for a while I felt as if I were on date with someone I didn't know or like very much, in a foreign land. But you have to move forward. I love my husband unconditionally, and I knew that there was no quick-fix for his condition. One thing that really helped me during all this was colour breathing. Focusing on breathing helps to increase oxygen intake, and therefore relieves stress and reduce anxiety. Colours have a psychological effect on our emotions, mood and body functions. So – putting two and two together – doing this exercise regularly enhances your awareness of colour, and therefore increases the positive effect it can have.

The colours to look out for are as follows:

- Pink equals love, compassion, and care.
- Green equals nurturing, balancing, and harmonising.
- Yellow equals happiness, uplifting emotions, positive energy, and fun.
- Blue equals calming and appreciation.
- Orange equals positive energy, optimism, and emotional expression.

Colour Breathing

Find a quiet space where you will not be disturbed.

Close your eyes and bring focus to your breathing.

Breathe long, slow, gentle breaths.

Feel the breath entering and leaving your body, feel the rhythm of it.

Visualise or feel your favourite colour pulsating in a circle, in the centre of your chest.

Feel it growing and expanding with every breath you take.

Feel it growing and moving in and around your body, easing all the tensions and negative emotions, nourishing you and comforting you.

Your favourite colour is expanding and penetrating every cell as it spreads around your body, transmuting all negativity to positivity.

Feel the uplifting energy it brings you.

Feel the comfort it brings you.

Surround your body with your favourite colour and invisibly seal it around you like an egg or bubble.

Visualise it or sense it sealed around you.

Sit for a moment and feel the safety of your colourful surroundings.

When you are ready, slowly open your eyes and come back.

This exercise is excellent, especially if you are doing it with kids. It helps with calming, as you can have fun, and they can have different colours and rainbows - which seem to be a favourite.

CHAPTER 8
DIFFICULTY CONCENTRATING

"In order to carry a positive action, we must develop here a positive vision."

Dalai Lama

Difficulty concentrating can be attributed to so many different things. If you are anxious or fearful, you don't concentrate well. If you lack sleep and restful nights, your ability to concentrate is reduced. Often, Mark would be unable to complete the simplest tasks, whether it was feeding the dogs, making a drink, or getting something to eat. He would start something and forget what he was doing halfway through. Sometimes, he'd just fall asleep in the middle of a task – like watching one of those battery-operated toys run out of power. I would often worry about how this could impact him outside of the home, for example what if he fell asleep at the wheel? There were times when, in the middle of a family conversation, Mark would be oblivious to what we were saying, as if he were unable to retain the words. We would have to keep repeating parts of the conversation, which was hard and frustrating. Then, he'd repeat things back to us that we'd already said. At first I thought he was taking the mickey, but the more it happened the more I realised the difficulties he was facing.

It wasn't just conversations that he had trouble following, but media too. When the TV was on, Mark would not be able to sit and watch one programme. He would keep flicking through the channels, watching snippets of different programmes and films. At first we'd laugh at this, even though it was a bit annoying – especially if you were engrossed in something and then he turned the channel over without any warning. But the more it happened, the more concerning it got.

To help us deal with this, we made sure we created lots of lists, put alerts on his phone and provided a calendar, all serving as reminders. I live my life by lists anyway, as it helps me to stay organised, but now we all got on board. Even small tasks that we previously took for granted went on the list, helping Mark to keep the day on track.

As mentioned, PTSD brings about major chemical changes in the brain. As a nurse, some of the signs and symptoms I was seeing in my husband made me question whether he had early-onset dementia. He would "cover-up" parts of the conversations or the fact that he had not interpreted or understood something that was said to him. Now, of course, I understand that PTSD is a complex condition which affects everyone differently. It was only when I really started studying and learning about PTSD that I realised Mark was displaying textbook signs and symptoms.

- Make a note of any tasks on which your partner is struggling to concentrate. How is this affecting day to day life for you, your family and your loved one?
- Have you had to change routines to accommodate this? What coping mechanisms have you put in place, or could you put in place, to help manage this?

CHAPTER 9
GUILT AND SHAME

"Love is of all passions the strongest, for it attacks simultaneously the head, the heart and the senses."

Lao Tzu

It is common for PTSD sufferers to experience feelings of guilt and shame. In Mark's case, as an army medic, many of his thoughts revolved around feeling like he could have done more, or as if he should have acted to stop things from happening. He did share a couple of examples with me, and my own interpretation of the events was quite horrific, so I can only imagine what was going through his head having actually lived these situations for real.

Every single person tends to look for ways that we could have made a situation better, but in reality we often have little control or influence over the way things turn out. The ability to rationalise is somehow supressed, as we struggle to come to terms with our experiences. Part of Mark's therapy involved exploring this phenomenon, and helping him to understand that he could not have known or predicted a certain outcome. As a soldier, you carry out your duty without thought – especially during an operation. Still though, this doesn't alleviate the constant "what if" that he carries around. The shame started to eat away at Mark, impacting his mood and the way he interacted with others. Even on the good days, he informed me, it would still niggle at the back of his mind.

As someone watching this take place, I often felt as if I should be able to do something about it, to make it go away or make it better. But, really, there was little I could do. I just had to be there to support Mark as best I could, to listen, and to not judge. If you are going through the same thing, or will be in future, then it is hard – there is no doubt about that. But there are ways of coping and raising your energy levels to the point where you can get through each day, one day at a time.

One of the best things I did for Mark, was to get him writing in a journal. Writing down how he thought and felt really helped, but at first he was reluctant. If you are in the same position, encourage your loved one to stick at it. Journaling takes determination and persistence, and a certain amount of bravery too – the experiences and feelings are still painful to recount. Then, of course, there is the worry over what someone would say if they found it, worrying over whether they will be judged, what people will think. For many people, this uncertainty is enough to prevent them from putting pen to paper. Just remember to keep encouraging, keep pushing them to show their inner strength. Don't forget too, that you can also join in. When I journal, it helps me to be in a place where I can help Mark. I can express myself without adding to his blame and shame. Scribbling away in my books helps me find peace, and if I am at peace then he is generally more peaceful too.

The Ho'Oponopono (forgiveness exercise) is excellent for guilt and shame. Ho'Oponopono is a practice that was created by Morrnah Nalamaku Simeona – a recognised healer in Hawaii. You can do it alone, so when the tears start you can maintain dignity.

I have included the exercise below:

HO'OPONOPONO EXERCISE

Find a quiet place and centre yourself by taking some deep, slow breaths.

Focus your breathing on your heart area, as if you are breathing in and out of your heart.

You can place your hands over the centre of your chest, if this helps you add focus to this area.

Create an image in your mind of the person or situation you want to focus on.

Simply say:

- I'm sorry
- Please forgive me
- Thank you
- I love you

Keep repeating this until you feel the time is right to stop (you will know).

You can do this anytime and anywhere.

Say the words out loud or in your head; it is the intention behind the words that matters.

You can also have a different focus for the exercise - different people or different situations - though it has more impact if you work on one for a week or so.

CHAPTER 10
LIVING WITH PTSD

"Ultimately there is no such thing as failure.
There are lessons learned in different ways."

Twyla Tharp

Seeing the Light at the End of the Tunnel

One night, when Mark was on his residential, he called me. He was in high spirits, and very chatty, which was lovely to hear.

'We're doing relationships,' he said, 'and I have some homework to do with you. If there was one thing about our relationship you could change, what would it be?' Before I could answer, he said: 'I would like us to talk and laugh more, and build a better future together, for us to have a better relationship...'

I looked at my daughter sitting opposite me. How could I say what I wanted to change, when I was so unclear about what I had? Our relationship was completely different now, and in truth I often questioned what it was, exactly. We had just been existing, two people cohabiting and sharing space, rather than sharing a marriage. There was no closeness or intimacy. My husband was, at times, a stranger. Even odder to me was the fact that he was having a session on relationships, but nobody had asked me or the rest of our family, even though we were the ones keeping him going. I did find out afterwards that families were invited to an "open day", but the cohort declined it because the timing was wrong. They were not ready to receive visitors and play happy families. I do understand this. Maybe it would have been useful to know this at the time I was asked to put on my "happy family" face!

'What do I want from a relationship...?' I mused. 'Authenticity, honesty, the truth about feelings. How does that sound?' I had to give him something. Looking back on the incident, I think I did okay. I do love my husband, and I'll always be there for him, but unless you've been in this situation it's hard to appreciate how tough it is. The experience, I think, is different for everybody.

After we hung up the phone, it dawned on me that perhaps Mark had finally started the journey towards recovery. Lights were beginning to turn on in a very dark room. He was excited, and felt hope and positivity, and that could only be a good thing. I was proud that he had jumped in feet-first, and in the space of 12 months had gone from Stage 1 to Stage 20. The only issue was that I had not really been a part of that journey. I was still at Stage 1, trying to understand and anticipate behaviours, watching and waiting for the "theatre" to recommence, so I could respond accordingly.

When I tried to explain this to Mark, I used the analogy of him starting a journey, whilst we (the family) were still on the driveway. He was confused. I could tell he was unsure about what he was hearing. Having gone through 12 months of therapy, he felt like he had all the tools, and he wanted to use them. I, on the other hand, had none. I was making it up as I went along. His response made me both furious and sad:

'In my head, I've told you everything.'

'You've told me nothing, and I'm not saying I expect you to, but I don't know where you're at!' I replied.

'I was convinced I've told you everything, so we were both at the same point...' he said, through tears, 'now I understand... we need to talk. We need to talk lots.'

I tried to explain to Mark that I needed to catch up; but to get to Stage 20 – where he was – I had to process the first 19. On his part, he seemed determined that we would move forward to a new future together, and he was so excited about that. I felt bad, but still proud of what he had achieved.

Coming Home from a Residential

As I expected, Mark's first day home was full of excitement. He was like a child returning from holiday camp, eager to tell us all about the things he'd done and experienced at the residential. I must admit that this made me smile, but things still felt strained as he readjusted to coming home. Luckily I was working, which gave me a break from the intensity of the situation. After the third day of readjustment, I gently asked if there was anything Mark needed me to know, which might make things easier for him and for us.

When I asked him this, he gave me a funny look. *OMG,* I thought, *I've added a layer of pressure!*

Trying to pick my words carefully, I continued, 'I'm not sure if you think you've told me anything useful...but you haven't.

You may have thought you had a conversation in your head, but we haven't discussed anything at all.'

'Why, what do you want to know?' he said, a little defensively.

'Well, knowing a bit about the programme...your triggers, your coping strategies, anything like that would help me help you. Don't forget you've been on this journey, and I'm still stood on the periphery waiting to be reactive. I've got no idea about where you are or how far you've come in your head and with your coping strategies.'

Following this, Mark went to get his programme workbook, which is affectionally known as "The PTSD Bible". We went through it together, talking about how PTSD impacts the sufferer's brain, and discussing his timetable. I was particularly curious to see how many sessions he'd had which involved discussing family relationships. *Not enough,* my embittered mind thought. But, in reality, I was being judgemental. I knew that there had been at least two or three sessions on relationships, I just didn't have knowledge of how long they were, or when they'd taken place. Again, I felt as if the way my children and I experienced Mark's condition was being put to one side.

When I explained to Mark that I had been studying PTSD, to gain more of an understanding about the condition, and that I had taken a crisis counselling course, he seemed quite shocked. He was even more surprised when I told him that as part of the course I had received counselling of my own.

'How long have you been having that for?' he asked.

'Quite a while,' I replied.

There was silence. Then, seemingly from out of nowhere, he told me in great detail about one of his triggers, the flashbacks this caused, and how this impacted his nightmares. Under ordinary circumstances, I would have been pleased for him to share with me, but this didn't feel right. To me, it felt as if he was telling me out of obligation, not because he wanted to. So, we put that one to bed, and I left the room for a while. I went upstairs, and started reading, all the while feeling horribly uncomfortable.

After that discussion, I decided not to push Mark anymore to tell me about how he was feeling. As the days moved into weeks, he started working again. His mood felt lighter to me. He had his sense of humour back, and had re-engaged with his routine, with the dogs and with the people around us. I almost felt a bit jealous, and a bit put out, even though this was what I wanted. I kept questioning myself, wondering whether my responsive traumatised state was holding him back. In many ways, I think I had misjudged how far forward Mark had come.

With all this in the back of my mind, I arranged a brief session with my own therapist, to try and give me some perspective. She told me that what I was going through was normal, that I was just readjusting. *Okay,* I thought, *just step back and observe, see where we are.* I knew it was not my responsibility to monitor Mark, and in any case it had been a good few weeks, relatively "normal" even, without any PTSD-related incidents. We'd just slotted back into our routine. But even that worried me. How could things be normal? All the promises from the residential that we'd had – texting, phoning, we will do this, we will do that...there was nothing. It couldn't just go away like that, right? We couldn't continue to dance around the subject, surely, but if we did then I told myself that would be fine, that it was his choice and his prerogative. The last thing I wanted to do was add pressure, but it was important for Mark to understand that if he felt isolated and shut out, it wasn't us that was doing the isolating.

POEM - Hope

You were my lover; you were my friend,
But PTSD took over in the end.

Faded away from your former self,
You've turned entirely into someone else.

I don't know who you are or how to connect,
I don't know how to help, how to react.

You are so distant; we are worlds apart,
Who would have thought such pain in my heart?

Where is my husband, where is their dad?
Where was the laughter, the love we once had?

PTSD such a sneaky disease,
It enters and takes control with such ease.

It changes the landscape and affects how you feel,
Tears your world apart, yes this is real.

I love you; I'm here for you, I want you back.
Can you hear me, can you see me through your life-hack?

There is hope; there is help if you know where to find it,
You have to be brave, for the road is windy.

Hang in there, old veteran, sufferer of PTSD.
Your angel will show you, just wait and see.

Caron Sanders-Crook

The crisis counselling course I took also helped me immensely. It made me step back, look at myself and my situation, and use the same techniques to help me cope.

We are not responsible for the feelings of others, but we are accountable for our behaviours and our emotions. This, in turn, can affect how others feel. We can choose how we react to situations. So, while I cannot influence or change the behaviour of my husband, I can control and change my behaviours, which in turn might create a better, safer, happier space for Mark and my family.

CHAPTER 11
THE MAGIC INGREDIENTS

"For me to get through the toughest periods in my life, I had to look within to find the energy to do it. I don't give up. Never have. Never will."

Jonah Lomu

PTSD will test your relationship in ways you could never have imagined. Unfortunately this is a hard truth of the condition. There is nobody in the world with limitless patience; no matter how much you love your partner, PTSD will test and push you to the very brink. With this in mind, I felt it was important to include a list of things which will help you and your partner to remember and aspire to, as you go through this difficult time. Mark and I don't have a perfect relationship, nobody does, but what we do have is love and strength in abundance, and it is these qualities that have got us through the trials and tribulations of PTSD.

Be friends first. When Mark and I first met, we just "clicked". It certainly helped that we had similar professional aspirations, and whilst courting we both served in the Army, and were deployed to The Gulf within a week of each other. We shared a unique experience, some of which was positive, but much of which was unusual and a bit scary. Whilst apart, we wrote letters to one another, and remained open and sharing – I believe this gave us an excellent foundation for our relationship. To this day I believe strongly in the uniqueness of our relationship, as I'm aware of many other couples we served with who have since split. Many of them we remain in contact with, and some of them continue to be of great support to us – as they can relate to what we are going through.

When your partner is going through PTSD, it can be hard to know how to behave. As I've explained, if you get too involved in dealing with the condition then you will only end up stressed and hurt too. But, when you love someone, it's almost impossible to step back and just watch them travel down the path of darkness. In this way, you have to find a careful balance, and I believe that acting as a friend rather than a partner can help you to achieve this. Be there, but respect your own feelings and self-worth. Remember that showering your partner with kisses, love and affection isn't necessarily going to bring about positive change. As partners, we can be blind to the faults in our loved one. As friends, we can take a more neutral approach, and see things for what they are. The sooner the symptoms of PTSD are recognised, the quicker your loved one can begin the path to recovery.

Give each other space. Although you are a couple, you are still individuals. I know people who do not like to be referred to as "the other half", as they feel they are whole in their own right. This opinion is beautiful, and I think the same way to a certain extent, but Mark and I do have a special bond, a deep friendship. Sometimes we don't even need to speak; we just know how the other is feeling or what the other is thinking; we are that connected. This element of our relationship has been severely tested. For a long time, I felt as though I'd lost my ability to tune into him. Mark was struggling, and for once I did not know what he was thinking. His inability to voice or communicate his struggles, or put a reason behind them, caused significant tension. That said, we still live and have always lived very independent lives. We have our interests, some of them linked, but most of them not. This variety gives us different things to share and talk about when we do come together. I refer to us being two parts of a whole, and we are also part of a whole family, dependent, interdependent, and independent. Although our jobs have led to us spending nights away from home and family, we are okay with this arrangement. We each coordinate diaries and keep the household running. I consider myself lucky that Mark will take care of all the domestic tasks while I'm away, and vice versa. In that respect, I feel we make the perfect team.

Leave the right way. When we leave to go about our day, we always kiss, hug and say I love you, wishing each other a good day and safe travels. On returning, we do the same thing. We rarely discuss each other's work unless there is a challenge we faced, and we need a safe and honest viewpoint. I think it's really important to try and wear a smile when you get home – the home should be a place of relief, where you can escape from the stress of the workplace.

Don't take each other for granted. One thing I can say about Mark and I is that we've never taken each other for granted. I appreciate every little thing he's done for me, and vice versa. Mark brings me a drink in bed every morning without fail. I don't ask for this or demand it, he just does it, and I love him for that. Likewise, I make a point of saying thank you every morning and showing my appreciation for this at times when either of us is away. I really miss it if he's not there, as it sets my day up wonderfully. When your partner has PTSD, you will quickly realise that all of the little things you once assumed would always be there, are in fact subject to change. This goes hand in hand with my next point...

Recognise that things won't always be perfect. When it comes to dealing with PTSD, patience becomes more important than ever before. Luckily, Mark and I have always had patience in spades - we've needed to, especially when postings put us at different corners of the globe. As I said, your patience will be tested to the limit, but a good way of dealing with this is to actually acknowledge the problem head on. If Mark and I are not feeling "synced", we just try to give each other space and acknowledge that we are at odds. Instead of snapping and disagreeing, we'll just say 'We're not on the same page today, are we?', and that's enough. We both know, and go about our business, touching base every now and again. By acknowledging the situation, we ensure that each of us is comfortable in the knowledge of how things are on that specific day at that specific moment, and therefore reduce the risk of "treading on the other person's toes", so to speak.

Understand that PTSD requires a different kind of love. PTSD will have a major impact on intimacy with your partner. Not only does it decrease libido, but it also causes isolation and emotional numbness, both of which significantly harm relationships. Being at "arms-length" can be extremely painful, especially when you are trying so desperately to reach out and connect with someone, only to meet with a brick wall each and every time. Thus, a different kind of love is needed. Mark and I have learned to love each other differently, deeply and on a soul level. Although I've always felt this way anyway, now I came to rely on it, to use it whenever I felt that our physical or verbal connection had waned. In times of difficulty, I would feel it, focus on it, and extend out to Mark. Eventually, things began to fall back into place and feel less fractious.

When it comes to your own partner, remember what attracted you to each other in the first place, and use this as a way to reconnect. Be mindful about showing appreciation wherever possible – to boost your partner's self-worth and self-value. Let them know that you love them, and that you'll do whatever it takes to help them get through this.

On the following pages, I have included a short list of some more tips that I learnt and that helped me along my journey. I hope they will be of use to you too.

Do

- Take time out for yourself, to explore your feelings.
- Signpost and steer your loved one towards seeking help and support.
- Seek advice and support for yourself and family - you will need it.
- Be patient - recovery does not happen overnight.
- Find methods of self-care, and use them.
- Tell your friends and family the truth. If they can't handle it, too bad!
- Be as honest as you can with your children. Don't forget, this is scary for them too.
- Keep a journal; you'll be surprised by how this can help to relieve tension.
- Understand that feeling overwhelmed and suffocated is totally normal. It's okay to feel this way.
- Have a plan for removing yourself from meetings, gatherings and parties, just in case.
- Develop a strategy for dealing with sudden and unexpected events; they will happen and can be stressful.
- Hang in there - remember to breathe deeply.

- Learn to love differently.
- Learn and understand what PTSD is about. This will help you prepare for some of the behaviours.
- Know that you are not alone.
- Be flexible.
- Be assertive; there may be times when you need to take control to calm things down.
- Reach out to someone you trust.
- Communicate, appreciate and validate each other and those around you.
- Know that I relate, and I am here for you.

Don't

- Feel guilty.
- Feel sorry. Be compassionate and empathetic instead.
- Shout and scream, this only makes things worse.
- Underestimate how challenging PTSD can be at times.
- Shut out people who genuinely want to help and who care.
- Let family or friends play PTSD down and bring on denial. They need to (nicely) go away and make their adjustments; you have enough to cope with.

- Get side-tracked by those who say your loved one does not have PTSD. Seek professional help regardless.
- Feel you are on your own.
- Give up.
- Be surprised when people around you notice changes. They may not say anything to you at first, but they will see.
- Be surprised if there is unexpected and unpredictable "wigging out", by both you and your loved one.
- Be afraid to laugh.
- Be afraid to cry.
- Be afraid to wonder, query, or swear, and everything else in-between. It's a massive learning curve - everything is normal.
- Badger or put pressure on anyone. Go with the flow, if you need to.
- Pass blame - it's nobody's fault.
- Barter or add conditions to get your loved one to seek help. You cannot make them do what they don't want to do.
- Forget to self-care.

- Can you think of any other Do's and Don'ts that may apply to you and your situation?
- Make a note of them in your notebook or journal.

CHAPTER 12
THE BRAIN AND PTSD

"The emotional brain responds to an event more quickly than the thinking brain."

Daniel Goleman

While trying to make sense of all Mark's behaviours and emotions, and trying to figure out how or even if I could help, I decided to study and take a course in PTSD Counselling. We can only help the ones we love when we have some understanding of what they're going through. In my case, I wanted to know why some of the reactions I was seeing in Mark seemed to be so extreme, or at the time what I might have termed "an overreaction". Of course, I say this with caution, as for the person who is experiencing these episodes their reactions are appropriate and genuine. I passed this course with Distinction – nothing like having a live case study in front of you when honing your skills!

With the help of my counselling course, I will try and give you my understanding of what happens to the brain when a person is suffering from PTSD. My course helped me put the pieces of the jigsaw together, although there remained missing elements, as I did not have the catalogue of scenarios and experiences that Mark was flashing back to. What did become very obvious to me, is that brain structure and function changes with PTSD.

There are three parts of the brain which link to PTSD and the responses and behaviours that we see: the hippocampus, the amygdala, and the ventromedial prefrontal cortex. I know, big words, right! I will try to keep it simple – that's why I put this chapter towards the end!

The hippocampus is situated in the brain, roughly in line with the top of the ear in what is called the temporal lobe. It is responsible for **memory function and helps us differentiate between past memories and present memories.** It focuses on the **surroundings and environment**. In people with PTSD, the **hippocampus is reduced in size,** which means its ability to know the difference between past and present memories is also reduced. So, anything in the present that resembles something in the past that is related to the traumatic event, can trigger a response such as a flashback, fear and anxiety. This is a problem for us as "onlookers" because we do not know the full extent of their experiences.

A good example of this was from an incident I had with Mark. We were walking down a fairly quiet street, when all of a sudden he stopped dead in his tracks and said, 'I need to go back to the car.' Once we got back to the car, Mark explained to me that someone walking past him on the street was wearing a certain jacket, which caught his eye. Suddenly, he was "transported" back to one of his operational tours, feeling as if he were actually there, which freaked him out. Of course, I tried to empathise with Mark as best as I could, but this is part of the reality of PTSD. Even if they do choose to talk about it and share with you, it still won't be the whole experience. For many people, this can make them feel like they are being left out in the cold, or that their partner is keeping secrets. Not so!

In most cases, the person does not know how to start putting their experiences into words. Mark would often say 'I don't want to open Pandora's Box,' which is a phrase that I'm sure many of you will be familiar with.

The amygdala is located near to the hippocampus, in the front part of the temporal lobe. It is responsible for **triggering emotional responses and regulating them.** The amygdala is part of the limbic system (which I also studied as part of my complementary therapies) as it **receives and processes messages via sight, smell, taste, touch and sound.** It produces an emotional response to what the senses pick up.

The amygdala is reduced in people who have PTSD, so ability to regulate or control emotional responses is reduced. You can probably see a pattern emerging here. This reduction means that the sufferer of PTSD can behave in a way which other people might deem to be irrational. For both the sufferer and their loved ones, this can be tiring. Both parties are on high alert, for different reasons, and this can often be exhausting, which in turn leads to mood swings and irritability.

The ventromedial prefrontal cortex is **linked to the amygdala** and is located at the front of the brain. It **processes risk, fear, and the emotional response to these. In people with PTSD, it is reduced in size** and therefore its ability to handle risk, uncertainty and fear is also reduced. This can result in extreme stress responses, anxiety and fear in everyday situations, and may or may not be linked to the previous traumatic experiences.

Bring all this together, and you can understand why some of the behaviours you are seeing are as they are. Everything is on high alert. This results in fear of getting close to people, because of issues with trust, fear of going out, mood changes, anxiety, anger, tears and withdrawal. Any amount of change terrifies someone with PTSD. Often we would plan days out, only for Mark to go into a flat spin and create an argument or tension so he did not have to go. Or if we did go, he would spend his time asleep, so that he did not have to engage or assimilate with what was going on around him. This was just his way of coping, but it upset me at the time because I did not understand why. I figured he did not want to be with the family, but in reality he was having problems processing the surroundings and the interactions with people and the environment. New places just made senses and reactions more amplified due to lack of any familiarity, especially when there was no "safe space" to retreat to.

- Has this raised any examples of situations, behaviours or emotions that you have seen? When reading this, have you had a "lightbulb" moment?

- Make a note of any such instances in your notebook or journal, as they may help you bring things into perspective and make them more manageable.

CHAPTER 13
AND THEN THERE WAS COVID

"I am always looking for the next challenge."

Richard MacDonald

In February of 2020, Mark came back from a week-long stay at a residential, followed by a weekend when he had to go for a reassessment and review as part of his ongoing monitoring. He'd had his medication increased, and he appeared to have stabilised somewhat, so there was hope for us moving forward. We seemed to be ticking along nicely, the sense of fun and spontaneity had started to come back to our relationship. We could banter and laugh as we did when we first met. Things were indeed looking up. We'd even started to plan for our son's graduation in the USA, and I'd booked myself onto a couple of "Human Givens" courses, to help me manage any behaviours, should the need arise. I did not want a repeat of the previous experience at the gas station.

Then, came Coronavirus, or COVID-19 by its scientific name. I don't need to explain what this is to you, as it is well-documented and at the time of writing the world is at peak virus awareness, but it had a significant impact not just on our travel plans but on Mark too. As flights were grinding to a halt, and more and more countries were going into lockdown, my son said he wanted to come home. We moved fast, getting him onto the next available flight. Shortly afterwards, the world went mad, or so it felt. The USA went into full lockdown, stopping all flights in and out of the country, and other countries did the same. Mark started getting calls for equipment from all over the world. He was working day and night solidly for about 7-10 days trying to accommodate for different time zones.

Naturally, I worried about Mark's behaviour. I could see it all unravelling before my eyes, eighteen months of therapy and settling in, undone by the stress of COVID-19. Many of you will already know the impact that lockdown has had on you and those around you. Now, just imagine that all the feelings of anxiety, fear, isolation, and the emotional highs and lows were amplified significantly. For Mark, who had just started re-engaging with the world, he was suddenly closed off again. He had difficulty being cooped up, despite our attempts to try and make lockdown as fun and engaging as possible. And then, things got worse. First, Mark got the virus, and my son too. Naturally, me and my daughter followed, and soon we were all bedridden.

It's fair to say that we've all found it difficult and challenging, but there is some solidarity for us in knowing that everybody else is experiencing the same thing. This is unlike PTSD, where the majority of people are completely in the dark about the issue. I think the whole COVID-19 experience has taught our family to stop and appreciate the things we took for granted before, and to re-evaluate what really matters to us.

During times of worry and uncertainty, I found that the "Inner Ease Technique" really helped. Again, this is something you can do anytime and anywhere.

The Inner Ease Technique

Practising Inner Ease generates a peaceful feeling and creates "flow" by helping to regulate the balance and co-operation between our heart, mind, and emotions. Doing this regularly will help raise your happiness levels.

1. When you are stressed, or your heart feels shut down, acknowledge your feelings as soon as you sense that you are out of sync (emotions such as frustration, impatience, anxiety, overload, anger, judgment, etc.)

2. Put your hand on your heart area and pretend you are breathing in and out through your heart. Breathe slowly and gently, until your breath feels smooth and balanced.

3. During the heart-focused breathing, imagine with each breath that you are drawing in a feeling of inner ease and infusing your mind and emotions with balance and self-love from your heart. (Research from the Institute of HeartMath has shown that radiating love and self-care through your system activates beneficial hormones and boosts your immunity.)

4. When the stressful feelings have calmed, affirm with a heartfelt commitment that you want to anchor and maintain the state of ease as you re-engage in your projects, challenges, or daily interactions.

Once you are familiar with this technique, practise it as many times a day as you can. You will feel the benefits and changes it brings, not only with yourself but with those around you.

Used with kind permission from Marci Schimoff. www.HappyForNoReason.com.

Original permission given from The Institute of HeartMath www.heartmath.org

Do this as many times as you feel you need to, but at least three times a day. Change the images or experiences you draw on; it will encourage you to appreciate them.

You can do this when you start your day, in the afternoon and before you go to bed; it will help you get a better night's sleep.

- Write in your journal the ways the pandemic has affected you and your family.
- How has not having contact with others impacted you? What did you do to get through the lockdown?

POEM BEHIND THE SMILES

I am me, and you are you,
We don't do the things we used to do.
We can love, or we can hate,
We can choose, so I appreciate.
We will come through, me and you,
We always have, we always do.
We fight on; we push through,
How? I don't have a clue.
Our core is love. It's strong, it's tough.
Sometimes it's all we had, but it was enough.
Things will ease after a while,
We will emerge from behind the smiles.

Caron Sanders-Crook

CHAPTER 14
B.E.E.
(BRIDGING EMOTIONAL ENERGY)

"Love is the bridge between you and everything."

RUMI

You have now reached the end of this book. Whatever stage you are at in dealing with PTSD, I really hope that you can find comfort and reassurance in my story, and know that you are not alone. PTSD is a strange and alien condition. It will change your relationship, your family, and your outlook on life. It will test you like you've never been tested before, strip you of your comfortable assumptions, place you and your partner in situations that you couldn't have previously imagined. But, all of this is temporary. You are strong. Your family is strong. PTSD is a weak and feeble illness, that prays on the darkest experiences, twisting them into nightmarish hallucinations. With the right guidance, support and care, it can and will be defeated.

Part of my reason for writing this book was not just to share my story, or to help others learn how to deal with PTSD, but also to spread awareness for this condition. At present, quite frankly, the human race lacks the medical sample size for us to know everything we can about PTSD, why it occurs and when it is most likely to flare up. What this means is that far too many people who have the condition exist in a state of confusion, as Mark did for many years, not having a clue about what is happening to them. So, I want this book to serve as a roadmap for anyone who thinks or suspects that someone they know might have the condition. It's fundamental that we put embarrassment to one side and ask the important questions. The longer you leave PTSD untreated, the worse it will become, and the more detrimental it will be for your relationship with your loved ones.

As you'll know from reading this book, for many years I felt entirely unacknowledged by the experts treating Mark, and in some respects I still do. While the medical community is still some way from perfecting our understanding of PTSD, this means that we are even further away from helping families like mine to manage the side effects of the condition. Therefore, books like this will prove incredibly important on your journey. As the partner of someone with PTSD, it's easy to feel lost, ignored, and unappreciated. It's common to feel inadequate, as if your feelings don't matter, and to experience emotions like guilt for even considering yourself at such a time. But, they do matter! You matter, more than anything, and the way you take care of yourself during this difficult journey will have a huge impact on the recovery of your partner. So, take time for yourself. Don't get trapped in the spiral of PTSD, which doesn't just seek to snare the victim, but their loved ones too. Using my tips, you can learn to manage your reactions to difficult situations, and avoid the numerous pitfalls that I myself fell victim to.

All the experiences described in this book are personal to me, and I appreciate that for you, things may feel differently. Now I would like to close by offering some final words in bridging the emotional energy gap between you and your loved one.

- Link signs and symptoms together to decide coping strategies. If you need professional input, or even if you are not sure, seek help anyway. It cannot hurt to gain experienced insight.
- Connect with each other, and together you will come through this. Connecting may be hard, but it's essential that you work together to break through the barriers that try and divide you.
- Join a support group or something that will nourish you as an individual. It does not have to be PTSD related. You may want to do something together, as my family did with camping.
- Remember the bond that brought you together initially. Draw on this and try to reinforce it wherever you can.
- Reach out to others who are in the same position, or who you trust; you may be able to draw from each other's strengths. A word of warning here: do not dwell on what is not working and re-embed your story, or you will take a downward spiral. If you maintain positivity, and look for positive focus and action, things will lift. There will still be down days, but on the whole, things will improve.

- Acknowledge and appreciate any step forward you take or any positive experience you share, no matter how small it may seem.
- Take inspiration from where you can, make notes and refer to them. Use them as a reminder, showing how to cope when things don't work out the way you planned.

Thank you again for embracing my experiences.

YOU WILL COME THROUGH THIS!

Resources and useful organisations

Caron Sanders-Crook www.caronsanderscrook.co.uk

All Call Signs https://allcallsigns.org/

Combat Stress https://www.combatstress.org.uk/

Mind https://www.mind.org.uk/

Royal British Legion https://www.britishlegion.org.uk/

SSAFA www.ssafa.org.uk

NHS Mental Health Helpline www.nhs.uk

PTSD Resolution www.ptsdresolution.org

PTSD in military veterans www.helpguide.org

Mental wellbeing advice for veterans and ex-forces
www.veteransgateway.org.uk

PTSD UK www.ptsduk.org

Help for heroes www.helpforheroes.org.uk

Phoenix Heroes www.phoenixheroes.co.uk

Walking with the wounded
www.walkingwiththewounded.org.uk

RM Mental Health www.theroyalmarinescharity.org.uk

RAF Families Federation www.raf-ff.org.uk

The Centre for Mindful Self-Compassion
https://centerformsc.org/

The Ho'oponopono Way
https://www.hooponoponoway.net/

There are also many social media support groups and local groups across the country.

Suggested Reading

Shimoff M. (2008) *Happy For No Reason: 7 Steps to Being Happy From the Inside Out.* Simon and Schuster. London. www.HappyForNoReason.com

Childre D (2010) *The State of Ease.* Institute of Heart-Math, 14700 West Park Ave., Boulder Creek, CA 95006; www.heartmath.org

ABOUT THE AUTHOR

Caron grew up in the beautiful County of Worcestershire and trained as a nurse at New Cross Hospital in Wolverhampton.

A Fellow and Mentor of the Chartered Management Institute, she has worked in health and social care for more than 30 years, as well as being an active member of the National Institute for Health and Care Excellence Topic Expert Group. In the latter capacity, Caron has contributed to many world-leading developmental and research projects relating to End of Life Care and Management, and Leadership.

Caron is an intuitive psychic medium. Her therapy, called E.I.G.H.T.S, (Empathetic Intense Gentle Heartfelt Touch Simplified) will be the subject of a future book, and training courses will soon be available. For more information, contact Caron at info@atouchofinsight.co.uk.

ACKNOWLEDGEMENTS

A huge thank you to:

- Wendy Fry for all her support and encouragement throughout this process; I could not have done this without you. Your Facebook group "Write From Your Heart 21 Days Journaling" was nothing short of inspirational. You are a generous human being, and I love you.

- Prof. Deborah Sturdy for your friendship and wise words. You are a dear friend to me and have been there day and night. Thank you.

- Richard McMunn, Joshua Brown, Jordan Cooke, and the team. Thank you for helping to make my dream come true.

- Marci Shimoff, Kim Forcina and the HFNR Team. You guys blow me away with your generosity, love, kindness and happiness. Thank you for being in my life, for the contribution you have made to it, and to other lives you have touched. You are a team of earth angels.

- Sally and Andy Bray, you are dear friends and have been there for us in so many different ways, thank you.

- Chris and Jaz Skaife, we miss you dearly. Dave and Kearstin Meadows across the pond we miss you dearly too. Much love to you all.

- Harwich and Dovercourt Rugby Club, a group of beautiful people who welcomed us with open arms, legs and beer glasses! We have had so much fun.

- Guy Harris, Joanne Bruce, Chloe Hawkins, George and Rebecca Brunning, and Annalise and Lewis Kerley, thank you for your support and friendship to Charlotte.

- Brandon Finch and Cameron Griggs, thank you for your friendship and support to Gareth.

- Laird MacKay, you gave me space and time when I needed it most, thank you. Amanda Rae for your listening ear. The managers in my team who do me proud every day. Saphrone Adams for keeping secrets. Alison Wood for being there and keeping confidences when I most needed it (you know when I mean).

- Nicola Raiman you are such a dear friend, your compassion is never-ending, you have a heart of glittering gold and are so wise. Thank you for your friendship for so many years.

- My family and our beautiful and hilarious dogs, for being there and helping us laugh our way through some difficult times.

- Charlotte and Gareth you make me proud every day, and I love you dearly. Aretta, Simon, Ella and Alex Hine - I love you all. We have shared and been through some crazy stuff! The pictures and messages the girls sent helped Mark and all of us stay connected, thank you.

- Everyone who has been part of this journey that I have (unintentionally) missed due to information overload. Thank you for being in our lives.

- Finally, my husband, who has provided me with a platform to learn so much about myself and others. Thank you. I love you.

ENDORSEMENT

Behind The Smiles offers a deep understanding of the signs and symptoms of PTSD along with the tools to effectively communicate with anyone who suffers from combat-related PTSD, to set realistic expectations, and to create a healthy environment for you and for them. The wisdom and practical strategies in this heartfelt guide will help you move beyond your own grief, helplessness, and fear so you can bring profound healing for you, your loved one, and your relationship. A brilliant resource for front line workers, nurses, caregivers, and family members supporting a loved one with PTSD.

— Marci Shimoff, #1 NY Times bestselling author, Happy for No Reason and Chicken Soup for the Woman's Soul